Online MARKETING CURATOR – ADS The TRAFFIC SOURCE...

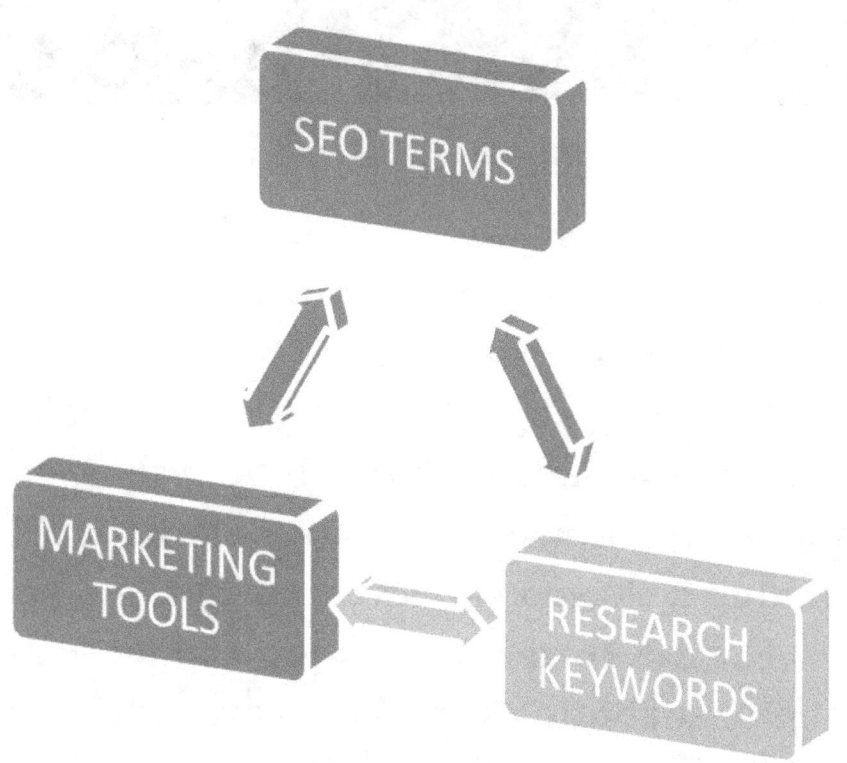

101 MARKETING SYSTEM

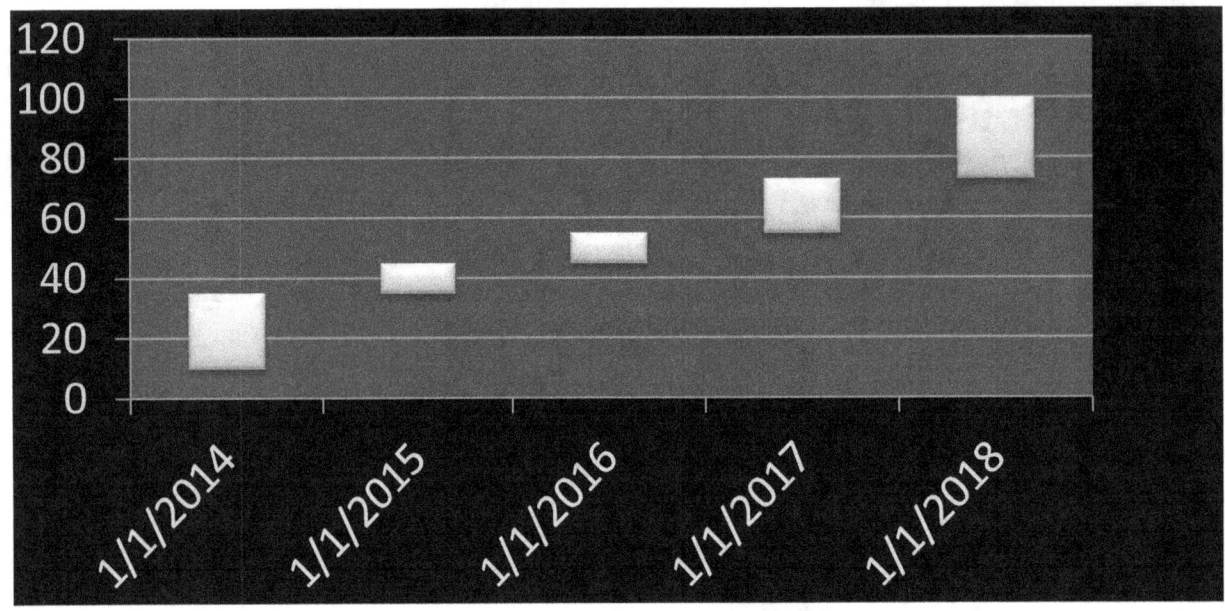

Thank you for taking a positive step toward improving and achieving your goals online. Trend information insight is important factor in moving your online business to a great height. In the following pages, we are going to look into the real actionable information that will help sharpen your marketing focus and improve your sales methods. These are eye-opening facts you can leverage and find your success online. The Ads format technique and motivational ideas are to help you build overcomer's attitude to write home greatness in your online business. Apply it and crown your efforts with success.

By Herbert O Nobleman.

Dreams + Passion + Action - Doubt = Success
This means that your ATTITUDE towards your
GOALS matters a lot.

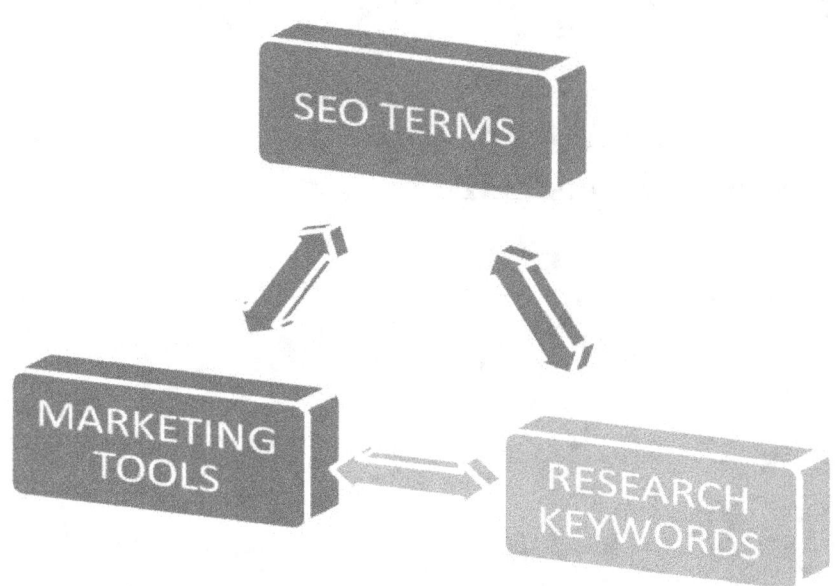

In order for effective and easy flow of marketing network online, the above terms are very important. The Marketing Tools are the mechanical part of online marketing. If they are not well fixed, the Marketing System will not function properly.

The SEO Terms are the Chemical part of it that ignites the Marketing System to generate sound [notification], which without your Marketing System will not be seen or noticed when the third part is applied.

The Research Keywords/Planner is the body/frame of the Marketing System that give guideline on where each item of the parts should be fixed. So these three parts of Marketing System are for effective marketing Network. Well explained below. Time for GROWTH is here.

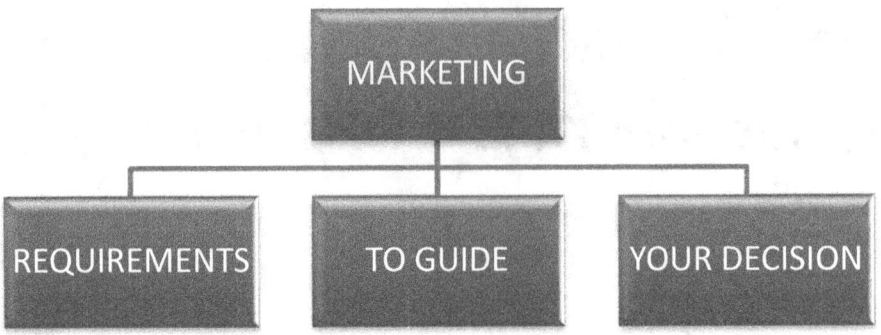

- **Marketing generally; both online and offline brings success when the following are considered.**

- Branding – This is the name, symbol, trademark or design of a product/service.

- Product Life Circle – Due to changes in marketing Terminology, when products fade out. This method [Product Life Circle] helps the company to manage the product/service from its creation till its demise, building a clear path for the upcoming ones.

- **Advertising – This is where the promotional tools/channels are.**

- Channel of Distribution – This brings the product/service to the reach of the people/consumers.

- Peoples Demand/Consumers Market - This is where the behavioral segment of the product or service is determined.

- So before creating your products or services you must consider the above terms

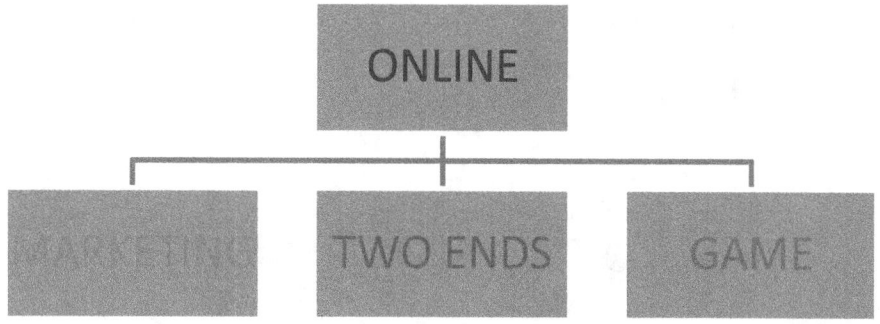

- Online Marketing can be more demanding because of the two ENDs it involves. Where we have the Front End [the ads you place online] and the Back End [the producer or affiliate that placed the ad]. There must be completely trust and honesty for success online.

- So this MEANS that:-

- Success Online is very much about matching in all things.

- Matching what you offer to what people need.

- **And also matching your passion and enthusiasm; to the needs, wants and desires of your customers in simple ways.**

- Success is about being the best you can be and knowing that you have served those who need what you offer to the best of your ability.

- Find them through honesty. Serve them with integrity. Listen to them with sincere mind. Grow with them in fear of God. Achieve your dreams through positive ATTITUDE.

- When you do that, you will have built a legacy, a business that becomes stable; survives you and one in which everyone wins.

- And that is perhaps the most beautiful thing of all.

- Your mind and believe make it possible or impossible.

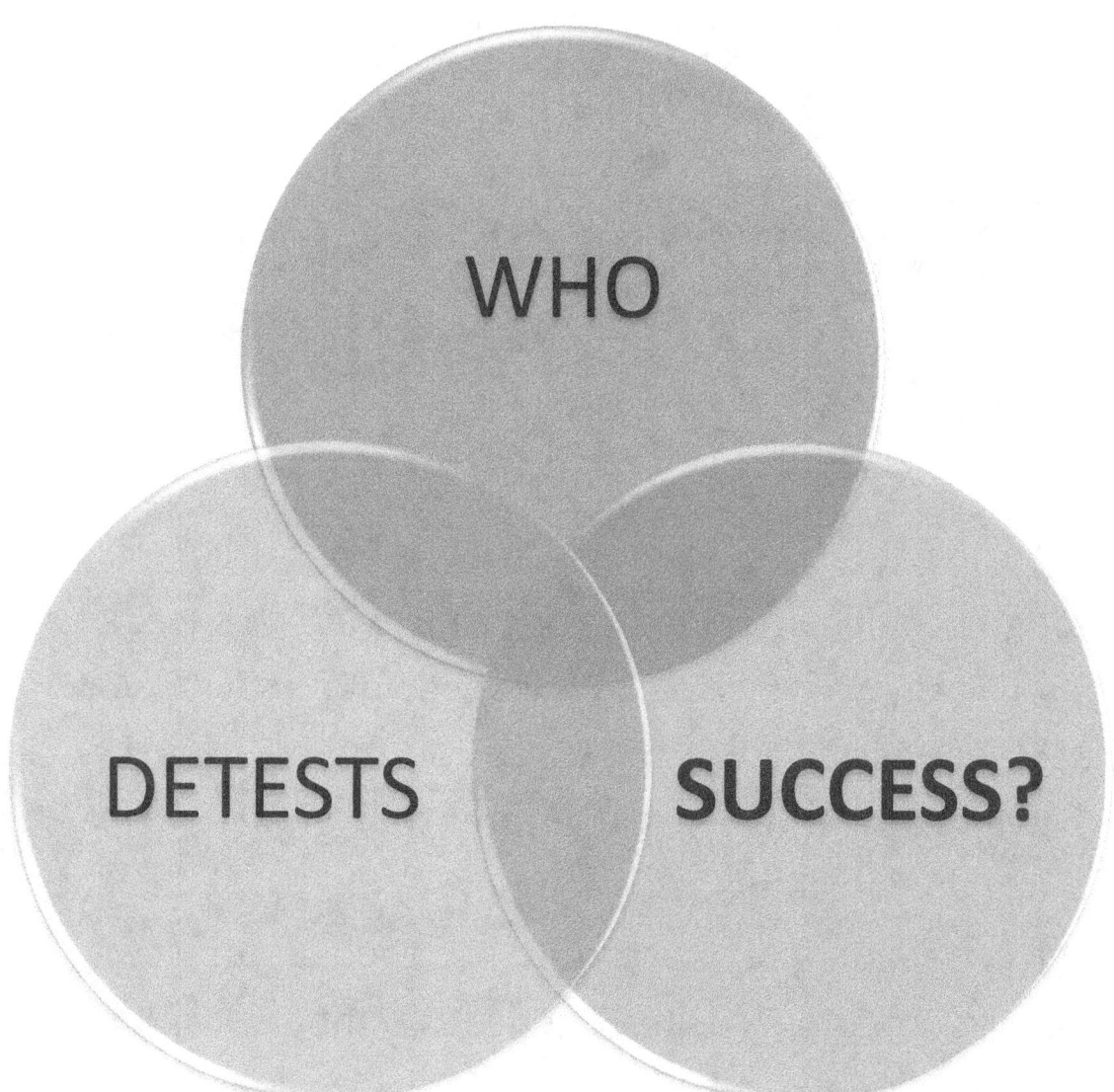

Like I said earlier, you can only achieve your dreams through positive attitude. If you really want to succeed online or anywhere else you engaged your activity, you must be honest.

Positive Attitude makes you greater than you're.

It will keep you above your competitors.

It will attract people to you. And it is the staff of victory.

Where your hardwork, intelligence and money can't reach; it will with Time.

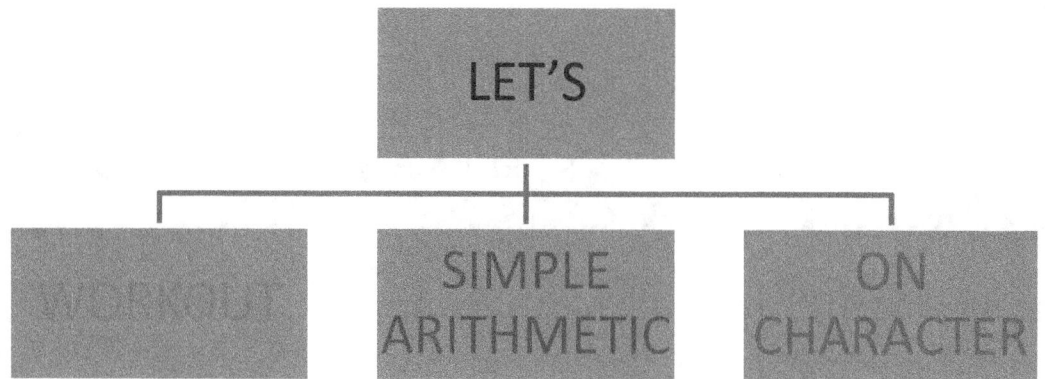

LET'S

WORKOUT SIMPLE ARITHMETIC ON CHARACTER

We have A – Z which is 26 in number right!
Let's assume that {A=1, B=2, C=3, D=4 etc.}

Let's calculate the Percentages of Hardwork, Knowledge, Money and Attitude to see the one that has the highest percentage. Or 100%, which is considered accurate.

Hardwork is [H=8+A=1+R=18+D=4+W=23+O=15+R=18+K=11]
Let's calculate: Hardwork = 8+1+18+4+23+15+18+11 = 98%

Knowledge is
[K=11+N=14+O=15+W=23+L=12+E=5+D=4+G=7+E=5]
Calculate: Knowledge = 11+14+15+23+12+5+4+7+5 = 96%

Money is [M=13+O=15+N=14+E=5+Y=25]
Calculate: Money = 13+15+14+5+25 = 72%

Attitude is [A=1+T=20+T=20+I=9+T=20+U=21+D=4+E=5]

Calculate: Attitude = 100%

The difference is clear. Attitude is very, very important to achieve greater height. Do not neglect it. Always follow the Positive side of it. You will win.

Don't allow 'I Can't' attitude deny you the beautiful result of your talent.
There is nothing impossible to a willed mind. This has been my Watchword.
And know that creativity, determination, and courage are the closest Pals to success.
The successful always sort different ways to overcome the hurdles of life and never give up when one door shuts.
But the failure is an orphan to the successful. The failure never finds anything good in others.
He believes that he is incapacitated in all things; hoping to get things all the time from people.
One thing you should know is, when you trust man and fail to believe in yourself and that you have been made for; you can never be able to stand the disappointment that will emanate from those you trust.

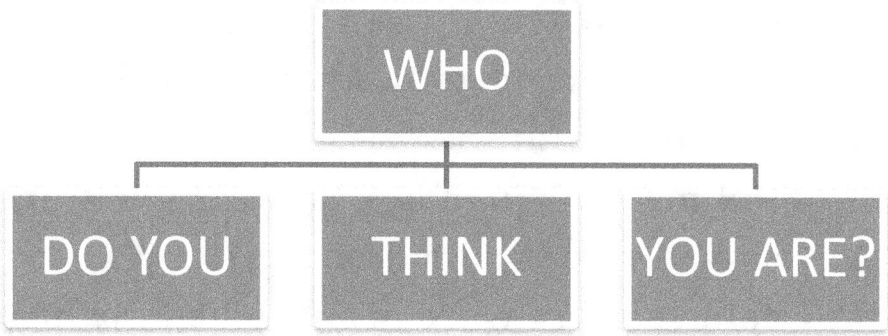

WHO DO YOU THINK YOU ARE?

One thing, I learned from all the successful ones I have come across is; 'the never say die attitude they possessed'.

This has kept me going even when all measures fail to yield positive results.

I kept on believing in myself that I am different from every human being on earth; I have a unique gift and talent that make me different.

I have a unique name, and the Almighty wonderfully and fearfully made me.

And I was created for a purpose not by accident; the Creator God, who thought of me before my existence had designed unimaginable things to establish me.

To be frank, these words have kept me going despite all I have been through.

I often cast my mind back to His Words and Promises in Jeremiah 33:3 and it reads. 'Call unto me and I will Answer thee and show thee great and mighty things which you know not'.

Take note of the words in color print, do you see the reality of God's existence and His presence in your situation?

Yes! He has promised me and you high and mighty things if we call. I know too well He will never fail because He is Holy and Faithful.

Why then should I put my trust in man who lives today and tomorrow he is no more?

Why then should I believe every word of his, when the heart of man is evil, and the thoughts continually wicked?

Why should I hope in man when everyone is driving to be ahead of others in terms of financial accumulation?

'No one is satisfied with riches and wealth rather the rich exploit the poor.'

Millions who called themselves 'failure' are the millions who always say 'I can't'; accepting defeat before an attempt.

If you fail to walk with your legs in your healthy state then how would you be able to run when you're sick?

I mean, if you fail to lay the foundation for your success now that you have a life; definitely it will be impossible in the future when you age.

So do not be intimidated by the situation and trials you are facing now but be courageous to move higher.

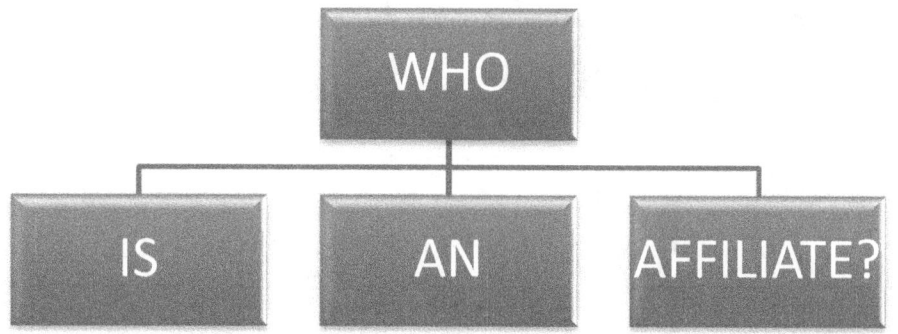

- With that said, we ought to know who affiliate is and what he or she does Online.

- **Affiliate is a person/entity that promotes; advertises or sells products of a company/person and in turn receives commission for his services.**

- Many companies/individuals have their affiliate platforms and their melt out commissions. Some keep to their promise and some fail. It takes Eagle's eyes to see these firms/persons who pretend to be Eagle while they are Turkey. So the more you promote good products the more your commissions surge.

- I explained the little you ought to know about the Internet Eagles and Turkey in my first publication on Internet Marketing Fact Files. Get your copy <u>Here!</u>

- And my advice is also listed in full, follow the honest people; find out Who is Who before committing your money.

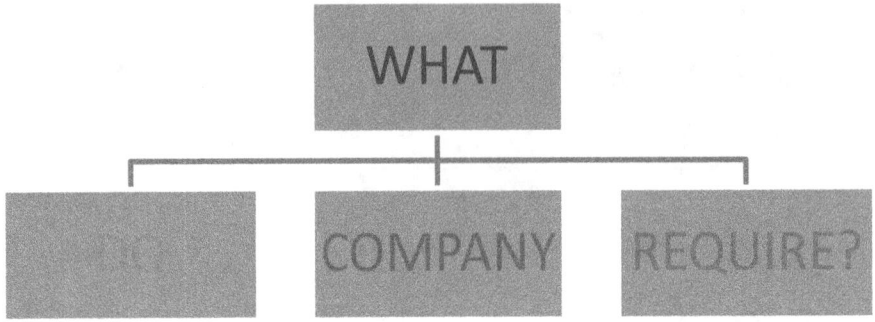

- **NOTE:** Some companies also require their affiliates to sign up with a token while some allow free sign up, depending on what they promote.

- But if you are an affiliate who wants to succeed online, and you don't have the economic empowerment; follow the simple format **blogging** though it will not be that fast for you to see returns.

- Patience and determination are needed if you must succeed using free sign up method. You must also have enough content to back up your promotional tools like your affiliate link, banners, and videos, etc.

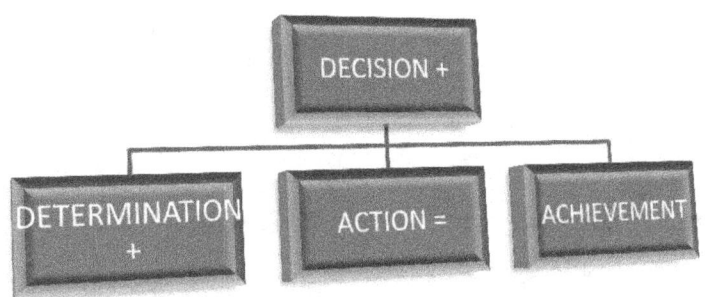

AFFILIATE MARKETING TODAY!!!

- Affiliate Marketing Does It Work?

- Affiliate Marketing does it Really Work?

- The questions we ask when starting; Or when we've invested much and nothing to reward our efforts.

- Real business is not Sow today and Harvest tomorrow. It must be cared for and nurtured to full grown business.

- Time is the only difference in this affiliate marketing business.

- We must understand that affiliate marketing is a real business, not something to, 'try'.

- The successful ones, who were persistent and focused, have laid a great platform for others who will come after them, people like you and me to succeed. And they have carefully put down the smooth staircase in step by step format to enable those that are ready, attain success; with little or no effort.

- Affiliate Marketing requires more information than what you can imagine.

- Information is the channel to knowledge and knowledge is the road to progress and progress is the step to success online.

- Make Use of the Information within Your Reach

- If you fail to take the first bold step; the second step will be too difficult and cumbersome to be lifted.

- Start with the little in your hand, head or pocket in due time, your effort will be rewarded.

- No one is perfect and only when you accept and admit that you need help, and then you will get one.

- People reject information, and they miss much a great deal.

- Do not discard information in its entirety; what you should and ought to refuse is the negative side of it.

- I don't reject information mainly documented ones, and I tell you the truth, I build my world around it.

- I know that I am not perfect, and my knowledge section is not filled; so I will continue to download more and more information to evolve with time.

- Information, they said, makes the world go round. If you believe this then, you have something that someone, somewhere ought to hear or know.

Methods of

GENERATING

TRAFFICS

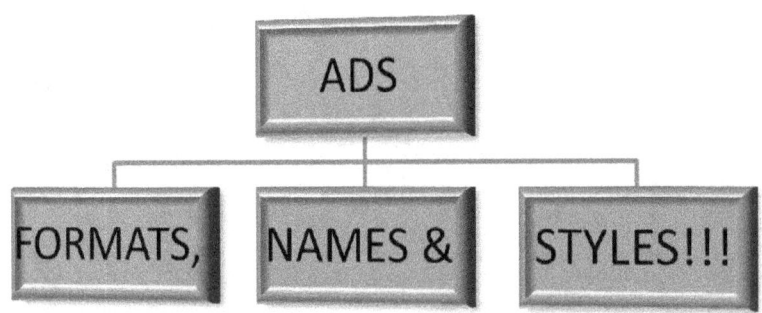

The Traffic Channels are the Key Road to Success Online Marketing

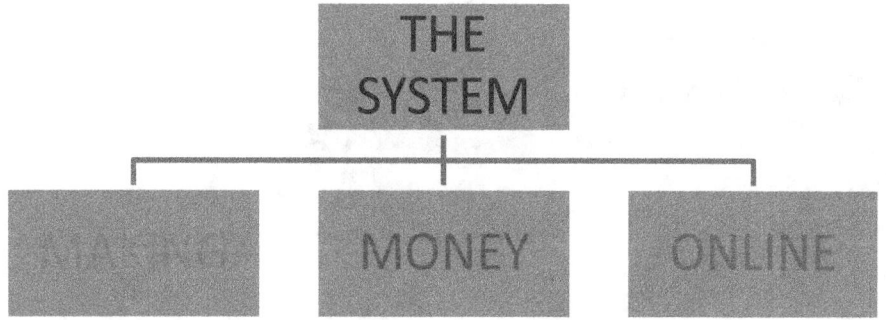

- Note that making money online requires these three things – I called Marketing System.

- Something to sell

- A website that makes the sale

- People coming to that site [called Traffic]

- The first and second required things above could be easy to acquire but the third is where the major problems are. People are the live wire of online marketing business. So I ask these questions –

- Can one succeed without TRAFFIC?

- Traffic is it the LIVE WIRE of online marketing business?

- We find out before the end of this Article.

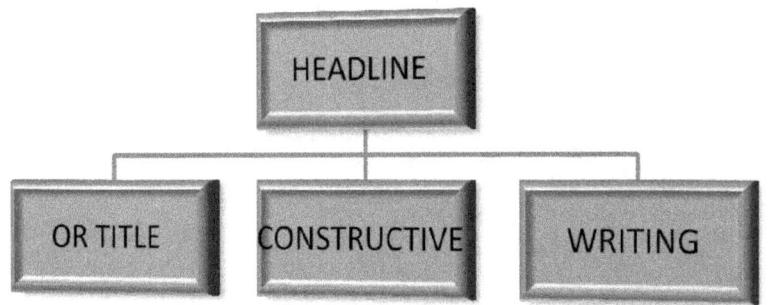

- **There are lots of things to learn; when one is starting any form of business, not only Online Marketing business, but also in other businesses. The fundamental TRUTH of such; is the key success in any of these businesses and that is why I said, anyone that wants to succeed in whatever he or she does, must be keen to information.**

- Because you cannot hit a target that is invisible to you, aimless shot means no target. And you cannot conceive what your mind has no knowledge of. So your expectations will be met base on the level of your knowledge, the more you Research and Digest the information within your reach, the more you will Grow in knowledge of the business you're in.

- You must do all you desire in the right direction knowing where you're coming and where you're going; I said this again and again. If not, you will never get to your destination, 'meaning your goals will not be achieved'.

In every **ADVERT**, there are things that matter most and which helps one to succeed in his campaign. And Online Marketing is all about creating the awareness of your product/service to millions who surf the InterNet. Some might have a specific product in mind or some might not. But the most important part of this is, how to attract them to that you're selling or adverting.

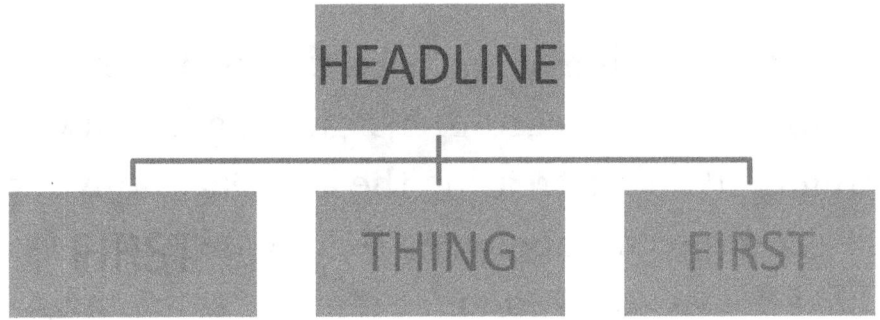

- Headline is fundamental to Online Marketing. Headlines are one of the keys to successful Online marketing campaigns. It should be the magnetic force that pulls your prospects or readers. It might be Solo Ad that is specific or targeted; it might be Content Marketing that also goes with the headline, Article Marketing, **Blogging** or Social methods. Whichever form, you chose to run your Ads, boils down to the same thing. Now how do you know **HEADLINE or TITLE** that will attract clicks and conversions?

- There are different types of headlines depending on your choice of usage. And I, personally chose to name them in this way:

  ○ Social Fact Headlines

  ○ Menace Headlines

  ○ Reward Headlines

Each one of the above headlines has a method that suits it and it must correspond to the body of your campaign.

Many use different headlines with different body contents to deceive the readers just like the INTERNET TURKEYS.

Note; honesty and integrity are the best way to keep your list members or your readers' faithful making them trust every word you passed across.

The killing tricks behind the successful pulling traffic on social media are better and intriguing HEADLINES.

Sure everyone wants something that will attract them without a second thought, and that is the work of well written HEADLINES.

This will also keep the conversation alive as your customers, prospects and partners on this media will engage themselves finding out more from you.

But some of the sites like TWITTER, LINKEDIN and FACEBOOK are full of information that I call information CHANNELS.

Mostly we often encourage clicks to our campaign site or landing pages, which require constant updates with content that will generate more clicks.

A content, that generates clicks, is not necessary to be a page; it might be content of Ten words, Eight words or Three line sentences and so forth.

You must also know that status UPDATE of some of these media loses value in no time. Especially Twitter update loses its value in few days, so if it did not generate clicks within the time posted and few days, it would never get clicks because Twitter updates has short life span.

So building a perfect platform on HEADLINE writing puts you ahead of others.

And be sure to go back to your headlines over and over before posting.

Testing the headlines is also the best way to know the one that gets more attention of people, and you are advised to use it over and over again.

Having well knowledge of HEADLINE writing will make you stand out in terms of:

Social Page Headlines

Blog Post Titles

In – Person Sales Communication

Book or Report Titles

Presentation Titles

And many more

By this, you will have people to say YES to your 'Call to Action' (CTA); more and more will be attracted to your niche with a genuine purpose of patronizing your products or services. Note that; it is your honesty that will make them ask for more.

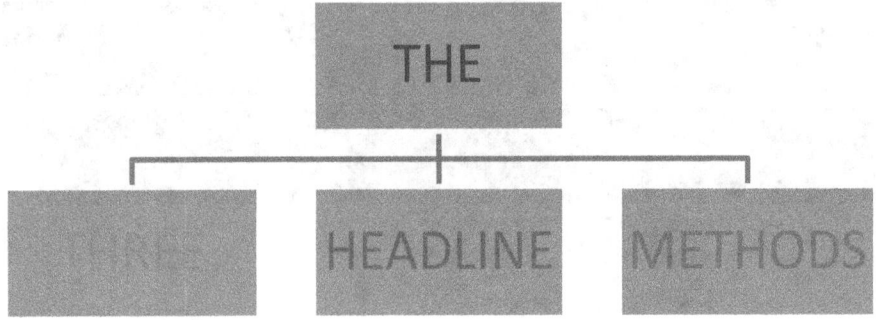

THE THREE HEADLINE METHODS

- Headline is one of the key factors to a successful Ad.

- Intriguing headline will help boast your ads.

- Here! three types of Headlines we are to talk about.

- As listed above, they are:-

- Social

- Menace

- Reward

- Let's take them one after the other.

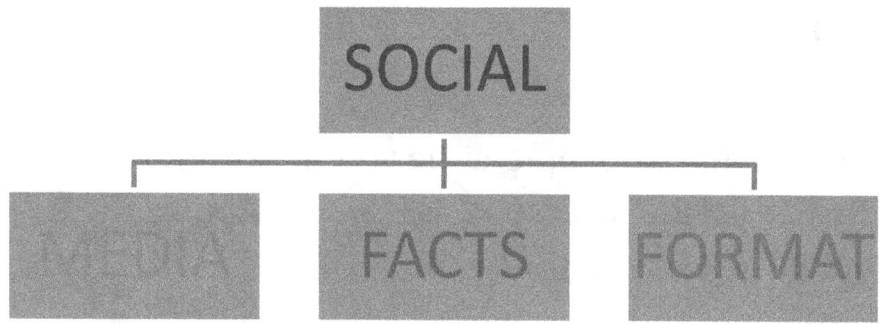

- An excellent marketing incorporates social proof base on the choice people make that resulted in others making the same choice.

- Human being generally, loves and wants what is said to be popular, in the sense of belonging to the happening group. So bringing in a headline that informs them about others been ahead in usage or attendance; they will eventually want to know why. Particularly with a well-known area with influential people; and then will the post attract more people to click to find out more about the information.

- Let's take for instance; one of the Mega Cities in your country as a venue where Indigence or particular set of people will have a get together on a specific date (i.e. why 1000's of Lagosians and State Security will gather in Sheraton on 27ᵗʰ May)

- Let's consider the name of well-known people; one of the ministers in your country. What he does after work or his diet or better still Lifestyle (i.e. What Senator Nziribe Reads At Night). People will be more anxious to find out the hidden secret, and then you have just gotten their attention.

Let's also consider the wants of people either on net or in their homes (i.e. The New Cure to Malaria Everyone Is Talking About/The Latest Smart Phone Everyone Is Talking About)

- The headlines have an Interesting Signal that attracts people to take action, just like I said; to find out the hidden secret is always what people are willing to do.

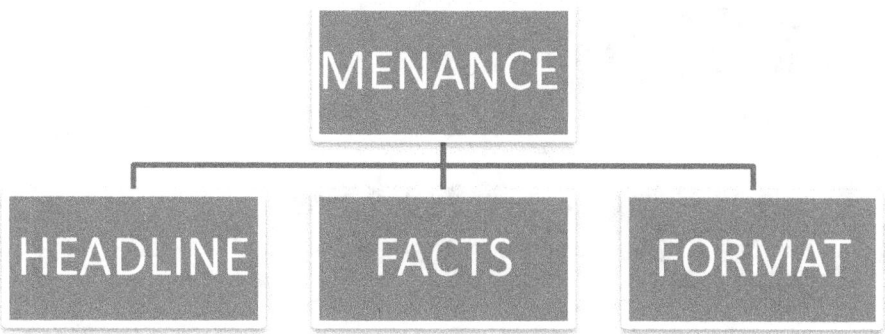

- This method of headline is the headline to put people in anxious mode and create a fear that makes the reader desire to know why. People fear failure more than that of success, so any word that causes doubt and fear are employed here to get the attention of people. Menace headlines like the following; create that burning desire to see the secret behind them.

- Why You Will Not Succeed In This Business

- Why Animal Flesh Maybe Dangerous To Your Health

- Why Cardio Workout Is More Dangerous Than Illness

- If You Fail To Get This Now, You'll Hate Yourself In Future

- These headlines are sure to get clicks because people want to know the solution to their failure, with a menace headline; the call to action will be **YES** all the way.

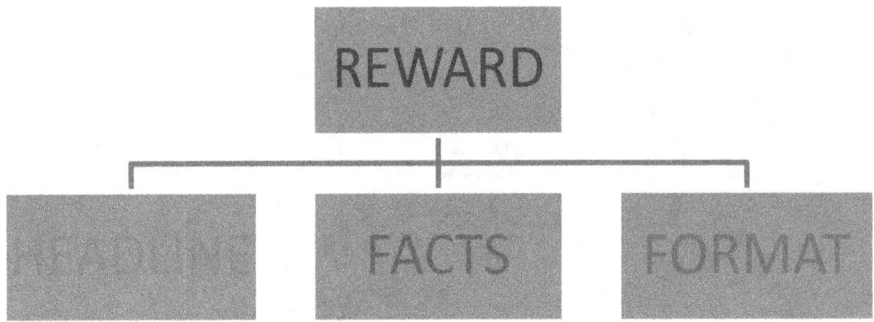

- This method also brings people to take action because of the benefits and promises listed which will be offered if they take action.

- People love listening to what brings gain, and they desire to hear them or see them often. So telling them about your company's products with the benefits motivates the response.

- How To Create A Website, You'll Be Proud Of Within 10 Minutes

- How To Install WordPress In Your Site With Few Clicks

- Sixteen Steps To Convert Traffic To Cash

- Simple Ways Of Saving Your Dog From Ounce

- Five Steps To Get Rid Of Your Stubborn Fat

- With these Headlines, people will always want more from you if indeed you live up to expectation by giving them exactly what your headline says. All about good and quality Ads boils down to the way your **HONESTY AND INTEGRITY** are seen in all you do.

Success is always there, but focused mind is required to direct your desires to it.

And you must also know that the Headline/Title is the manifestation of the BODY/CONTENT of you Ads in sentence.

Like I said earlier, don't use a different headline with different content in the name of making money or deceiving people to click or visit your website.

You can only deceive them clicking to find out what you have, but you won't force them to buy from you, so be honest to gain peoples' trust.

Get our First Publication on this Here..

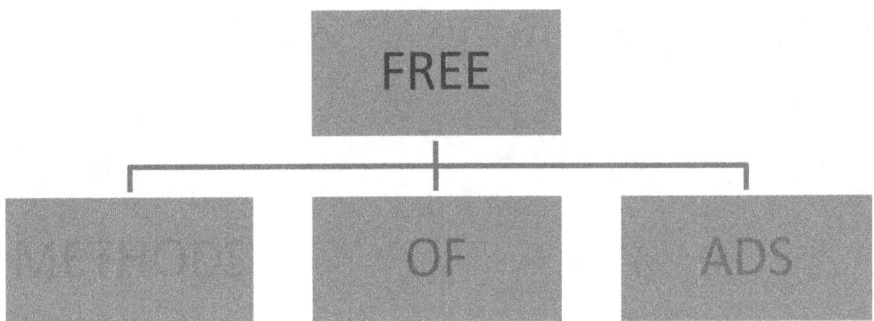

- **Advertisement** – called **ADS** are the channels through which you create the awareness of your products or products of the company you're representing as an Affiliate. So the two listed methods of generating traffic below are used to reach the prospective clients or customers.

- **There are two traffic methods of Ads :– Free, which requires your energy time and creativity,**

- **And Paid that you leverage other people platform to run the ads.**

- **Free Traffic – These are free channels or platforms in which we advertise or reach our intended customers.**

- **It is slow in reaching the prospective customers**

- **It takes more time than the paid to generate income**

- **It requires determination and regularly updates**

- **It works much better and fast in terms of returns when you have a LIST of your own – so starting is often the problem.**

Now here are the Free Traffic channels below: -

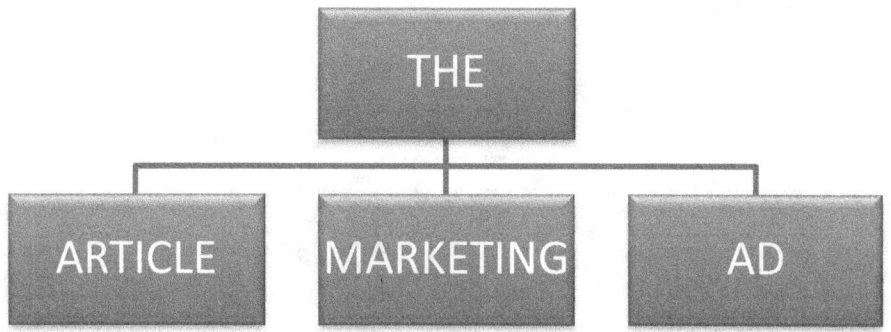

- Article Marketing –This is magnificent form of creating the awareness of your niche or products. Article marketing is all about revealing the problems that people face in life.

- Stating clear the causes and telling them how to solve it or prevent it.

- It does not need thousand words – at least in an explicit statement or language and to the point; 400 or 500 words are ideal.

- If you have written a descriptive essay, you can write an article that will captivate your readers to ask for more. But you have to be honest if you want them to trust you.

- Sites, you can post your free Articles, are **EzineArticles.com or Goarticles.com, etc.**

- **Get <u>EBook on this Article Internet Fact File</u>**

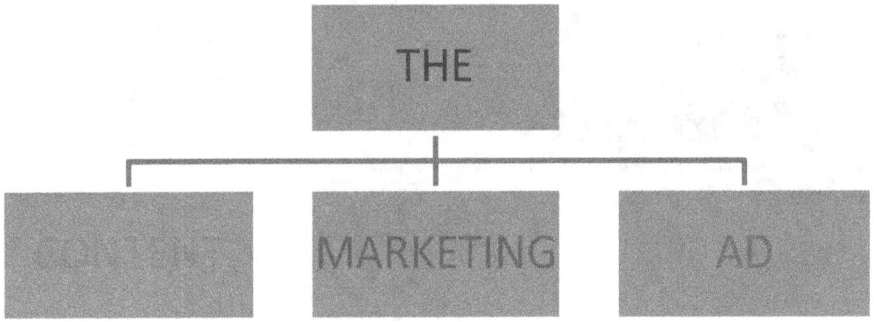

- **Content Marketing** - This method of generating traffic does not require many words like Article marketing.

- In an article, you only use it to build the trust and confidence of your readers.

- You don't necessary pitch in article marketing, but bringing them to your site not so with content marketing.

- Here you pitch that you represent with few words.

- Content marketing does not need a page or more before it could generate clicks or get the attention of your customers.

- A well-written content is that with captivate headline or title.

- The main body explains the benefits that the person will get if they do what you want them to do.

- And not by a force but willingly - and follows will be the persuasive method for them to take action in their own best interest.

SEO – TIME TO SUCCESS

If you're new to this industry or online marketing in general, you've likely heard about Search Engine Optimization (SEO). In a Community where the majority of traffic Resources stems from a string of text typed into a search box, the search engine can be a deciding factor in the fate of your business.

One of the foundational tactics of SEO is Keyword Research. Keyword research is the simple art of better understanding the terminology your potential customers are using to find the products you're selling, then matching your website and marketing terminology. You can use the following tools for Keyword Research

https://adwords.google.com/select/KeywordToolExternal
http://www.keyworddiscovery.com/search.htm

How Does It Work? Right!

One of the most powerful ways to use these tools and expand your keyword opportunities is to simply TAKE a very BROAD word and TYPE it in and see all the variations that people are searching for.

For example, if you just type in 'abs', you'll see all of the variations that people are searching for expanded base on ABS. Examples: - 'abs flat' 'abs belly fat' 'abs stomach flat' 'abs fat burn' etc.

It makes it easy understanding the words people use when searching for Abdominal Fat Burn, workouts or Dietary.

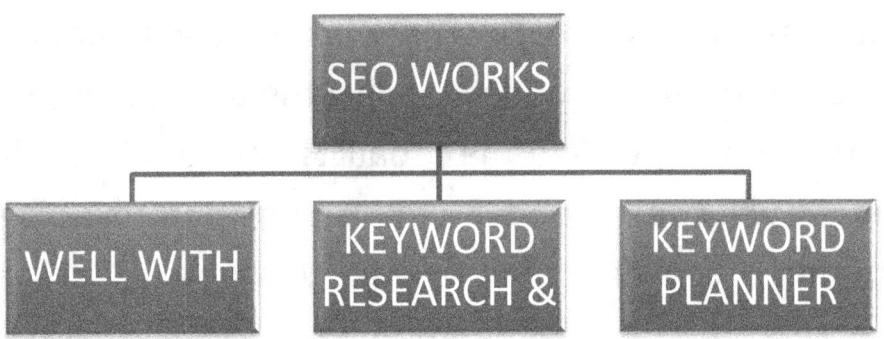

Another one like the Keyword Research is Keyword Planner. This works slightly different from Keyword Research Tools. You can search for keyword and ad group ideas, get historical statistics, see how a list of keywords might perform, and even create a new keyword list by multiplying several lists of keywords together. A free AdWords tool, Keyword Planner can also help you choose competitive bids and budgets to use with your campaign. Type http://www.adwords.google.com/keywordplanner into you address bar. Or click – you will be asked to sign in to your Adwords account.

To access Keyword Planner, sign in to your AdWords account at https://adwords.google.com. Click the Tools drop-down menu and select "Keyword Planner." If you don't have an AdWords account you can create one by clicking Sign Up button.

You can also use Keyword Planner to:

Research keywords. Need help finding keywords to add to a new campaign? Or, maybe you want to find additional keywords to add to an existing campaign. You can search for keyword and ad groups ideas based on terms that are relevant to your product or service, your landing page, or different product categories.

Get historical statistics and traffic forecasts. Use statistics like search volume to help you decide which keywords to use for a new or existing campaign. Get forecasts, like predicted clicks and estimated conversions, to get an idea of how a list of keywords might perform for a given bid and budget. These forecasts can also help guide your decision on which bids and budgets to set.

It's important to keep in mind that while Keyword Planner can provide some great keyword ideas and traffic forecasts, campaign performance depends on a variety of factors. For example, your bid, budget, product, and customer behavior in your industry can all influence the success of your campaigns.

Try it out here: http://www.adwords.google.com/keywordplanner

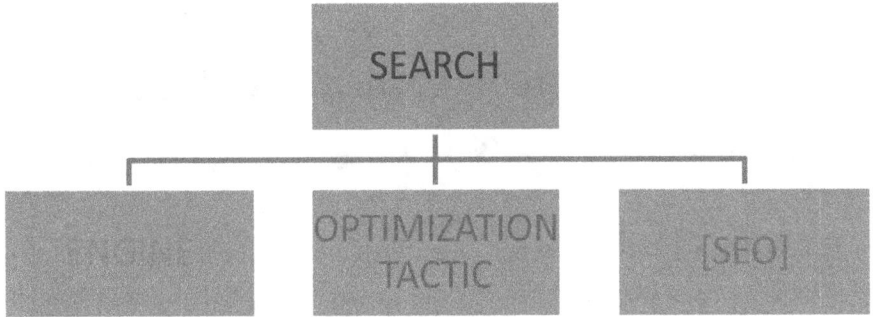

-         This is one of the best ways to create the awareness of your products or niche to the public.

- The tactic here is that our sites get listed in the venerated top ten search results.

- In this case, we can't trick the search engine like <u>Google, Yahoo,</u> etc. –

- So best way, we can be lucky, is to provide reach content website.

- Your site must be helpful to people and have more quality information.

- In this method, the organism called crawler picks sites rich contents at random, so quality content is required here as we said earlier.

- Helpful information for people is all that is needed. But not all is considered.

- **For a successful SEO campaign, use the two explained TOOLS above – Keyword Research and Keyword Planner.**

Get eBook Online Marketing Fact File

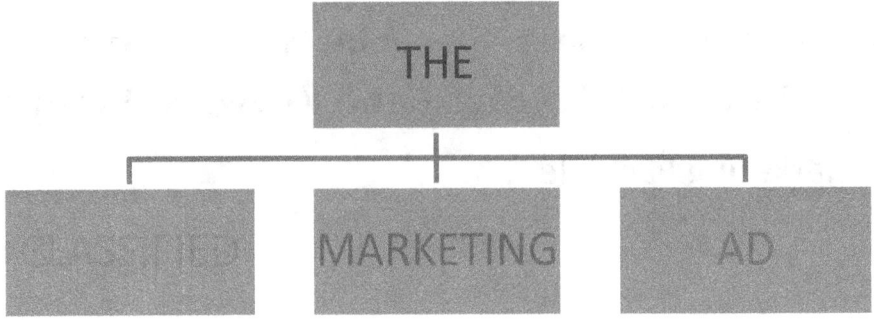

●**Classified Ads** –This is another method you can use to advertise your products.

●This does not work out easily like others; it might or might not function out, so it is mixed act in terms of results.

●You might be lucky to get sites that sale ad like classified Ads; so you're advised to adopt every means possible to your online success.

●Classified Ads needs not a page to be able to generate clicks or sells. See Example below..

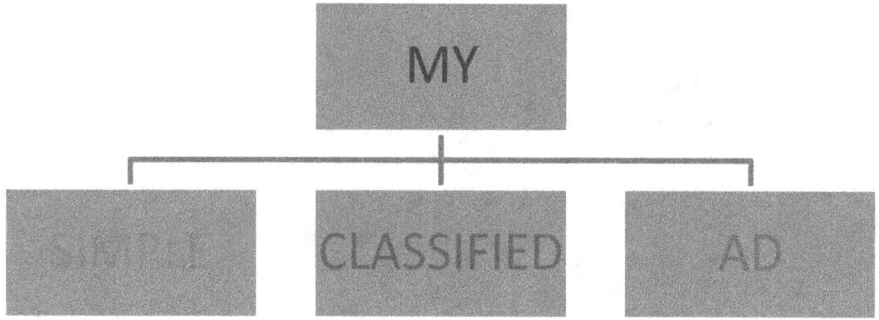

Making Money Online

- The Body/Content as Follow: -

- Do you need to create a powerful INCOME fast?

- Tired of the HPYE and high pressure and just want facts about MAKING MONEY ONLINE?

- Want to bring back financial stability in your home?

- I was there too and find a real SOLUTION.

- Here is YOUR Turn! http://noble1s.blogspot.com

- That's simple Classified Ad in Question Format above!

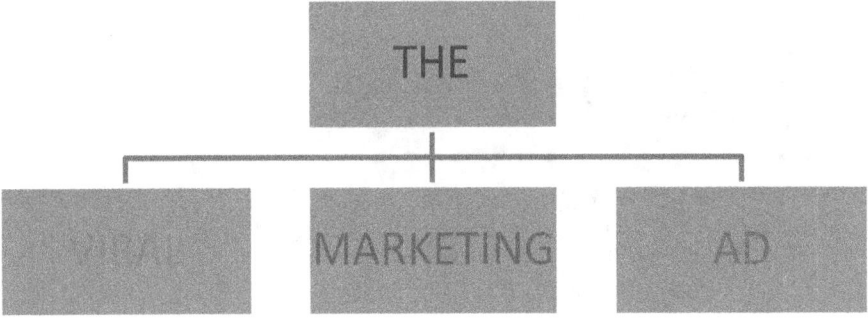

- Viral Marketing – This is another method one can attract customers through the use or means of this statement; 'use that in your hand to get that you want.'

- Example; You want customers to come to your site to buy your products or what you offer, and you don't have a list of your own.

- Then you assigned one of your products to a particular list owner to give to his or her list members for **FREE –.**

- Through this method the list owner will be able to provide a quality information or product out for FREE gaining trust from his list members.

- And you the owner of the product have your link in the product you gave to him; that for sure, the customers interested in what you offer will visit your site for the product.

- So it's all gain and win - win game. The best product or commonest of this; is small **E – book or Software**

- **Blog Publishing** – This is super charge among all the other Free Traffic Methods.

- Why? Because you have the right to design it to your taste; it is basically the same as a website.

- When the blog site is rich with great content, the search engine and people will pick note of it.

- The advantage to a blog is that you can have some interactive moment by letting people comment.

- It can be structured in a way that it will be easy for people to read – plus, you can offer an RSS feed for those who prefer that method of getting content automatically.

- With rich content in a blog site like Blogger; 'You might be lucky to get Google Trust in Placing Ads on your blog post through Adsense – which puts money in your pocket when those Ads generate clicks.

- Blog Site you can visit are: Blogger.com, Weblog.com, webly.com, wordpress.com, tumblr.com, etc.

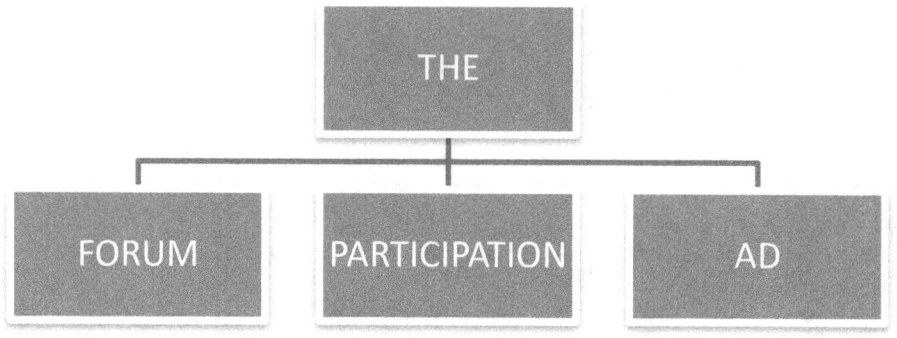

- Forum Participation – This method is both for learning and selling your ideas.

- Participating in forums helps you share your knowledge and also obtain knowledge through the questions and answers offered by the forum.

- But your focus must not be in selling or advertising your products rather it should be means of buying the trust of people in that forum.

- Many people have made much through this medium because of their honesty. Forums like LinkedIn, Joint Venture, and Warrior Forum, Warrior Plus, etc.

- But if you have more time than money at this point in your life these techniques will work to get traffic to your site.

- Ezine Article Publishing – Is highly profitable and easy to do.

- All, you have to do, is to gather information on a particular subject that could be of people's interest; write about it and create the awareness through free ads publication like ezines, etc.

- If you want to get more traffic to your site, it is advice that you publish it free, and when the traffic surges, then you can decide to sell when you must have built your list.

With that said on Free Traffic method – which I call the Invisible Leadership where one stays in lonely hours, toils in his or her craft behind closed doors.

No one celebrates it; even you might be mocked, teased and ridiculed by your friends and family.

The inside critics fire off heckle as soon as you begin – fears, discouragements and doubts if what you are doing will ever work or pay or reward your efforts.

Yes, no one pays for that in fact it cost time, energy and often money.

But the joy comes when the seeds you sow in silence and tears and pains eventually produce a public harvest greater than you can imagine.

Traffics begin to flank, and money begins to surge as many demands your products. This is mostly invisible at the beginning but visible through your achievements. Repeated!

So stay focused and finds the very possible ways to achieve your online dreams.

Get Ebook on this Article Internet Fact File

Get More to help you achieve more – ClickBank Programs

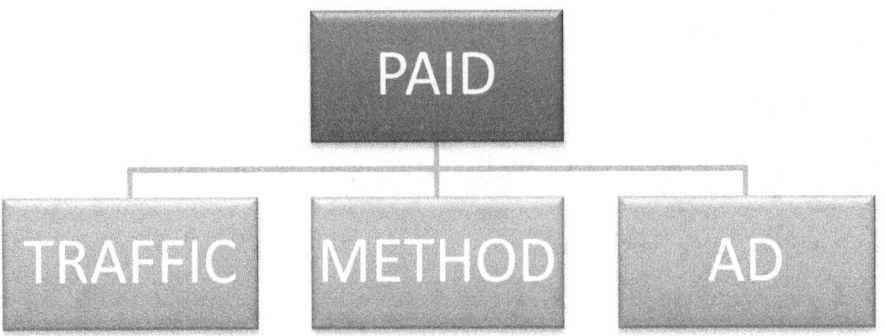

- Just like the Free Traffic methods, the paid ones are different in a trace – that means they are close related.

- Both are **PAID** differently; Free Traffic is paid through our efforts as we said earlier while the Paid Traffics are paid from our pockets.

- So let see some of the Paid Traffic Methods.

- **Paid Traffic Methods:** - The means we leverage a person's or company's platform/ad tools to reach our prospective customers through ads and in turn get traffic back to our sites.

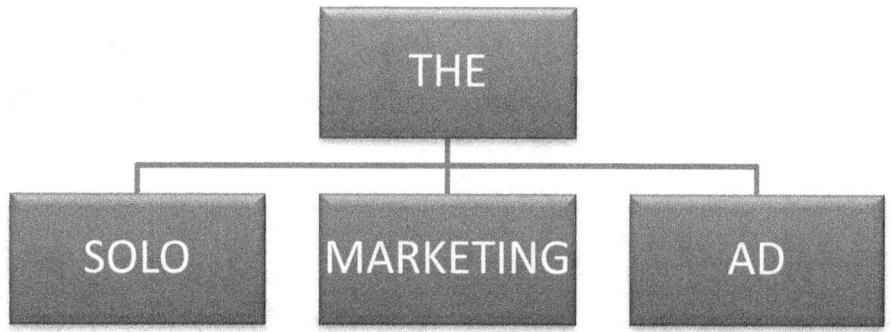

- **Solo Ads** – This works out when you have a trusted partner or platform that has a list. It requires you to run your ads on someone else's email list.

- You have to agree with the owner of the list of the numbers of clicks he or she has to deliver.

- It might be 5,000 clicks for $100 or more, depending on your pocket, and the money will be paid when the clicks complete.

- Though some might not fulfill their promise by producing the right clicks – it might be 2,500 genuine and 2,500 spams, which is the bad side of this method of generating traffic.

- But you are advised to request Solo Ads from forums you belong, like LinkedIn, Joint Venture, and Warrior Forum, etc.

- Because they will monitor the transactions to make sure that the list owner delivers 100% before his or her money will be paid.

- The good side of this type of Ad is that it's targeted. But not all clicks will be converted to money. It's called Solo because just one Ad will be run at a time till the clicks completed.

- Email Swaps - This should be FREE not PAID method. It is always profitable if done in an honest way.

- It is like the first one we discussed **'Solo Ads'.**

- But the only thing is that you don't have to pay a dime, but you will reach an agreement with the other party to swap email lists, if you have a list.

- Where you don't have a list, you will pay. If you have hundred members list and your partner has **100 – 500** it does not matter, what matters is your own list.

- The idea is; you have run several ads on your list with your products and you want to reach to other people in other lists owned by someone else to create the awareness of your products.

- All you have to do is to find the list owner who will agree to swap Email with you.

- When you run his ads in your list, and the hundred clicks completed, he will in turn runs your ads in his list for hundred clicks also.

- Through this medium, you have been able to advertise your products in his list and his in yours – that is what Email Swap is all about.

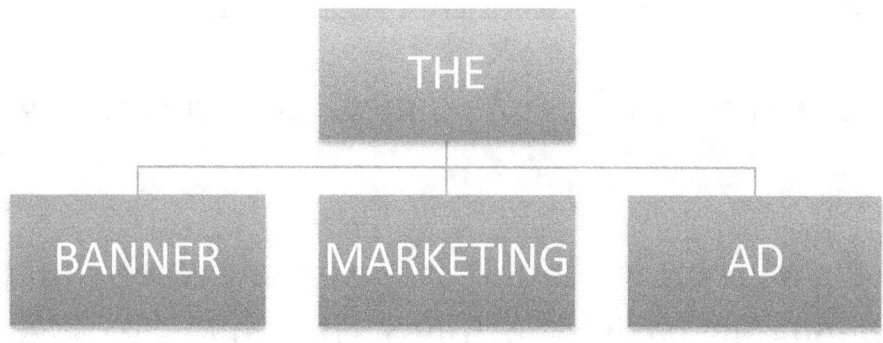

- Banner Ads - It requires a platform or company that runs banner ads on their websites.

- So you have to find a site that accepts banner Ads and reach agreement and note that your banner must have your site link encoded or your affiliate link – with a descriptive writing of your product.

- Social Media –This requires you to create a page in the social media like <u>Facebook</u>, <u>Google Adwords</u>, <u>LinkedIn,</u> etc.

- Facebook has been the Firefox in this method of generating traffic.

- Once you have a page on Facebook, it is easy to create your ads, and after your ads have been approved, you be charged Per click [CPC – Cost Per Click] as your ad runs.

- This I called untargeted traffics; getting tons of traffics and making small or no sales.

- **Direct CPV & Media Traffic** – This method is the best among the paid traffics- why? It is direct and targeted traffic. Targeted I mean here is the buyers through the search engine results. Yes, it's about the buyers online for the product you're advertising. Your site will be shown to them through DPV Network.

- You can add as many as the URLs that search engine listed based on the product or company you are advertising.

- So any of the buyers from Google, Yahoo, etc. that types in the keyword of your product, website or company; automatically, your URL will be shown to him or her.

- What we are talking about here is not clicks, but one who is ready to buy at that moment.

- To get the search engine results like Google you have to use these signs in Keyword Search Box [=, +, _,20%, *, &]

- For example, If you want to search for top URL for your product or company. Using the keyword permutations [i.e. health and fitness] =health+fitness_weightloss] health*fitness*diet] health&fitness&anything you want to add to it pertaining on your niche.

- The more you use the keyword search permutations the better.

- The Key word search will be [http://www.google.com/#hl=en&q=health+fitness+weightloss&aq=&aqi=&aql=&oq=&gs rfai=&pbx=1&fp=854fbacba92654cf] this exactly how Google results will look like.

- And the results will be what you will use for your DPV. That is why I said it is the best method - send less and sale much. And you must have account with Direct CPV before you usage.

- So if you keep the keywords or Url targets which must aimed at the buyer in that niche you're; it will definitely produce much than you can imagine.

- This one is bigger than what we can treat here. Want more on this, let's have you set right <u>Here!</u>

- These articles are targeted email Ads.

- In the sense that the football lovers will love to read football articles, golfers will like to read articles base on golf also, and those seeking weight loss will be interested in that niche.

- So for best results on this method of traffic, you have to find out the person that has a list on the niche you are promoting.

- If your company's product is in health & fitness; you're strongly advised to focus on that by checking the categories of the **Ezines publishers.**

- And find out the one that has list of people interested in health and fitness.

- It's more profitable than publishing it on a list of different choices and wants.

  Note that targeted traffic is the most beneficial in this industry or business.

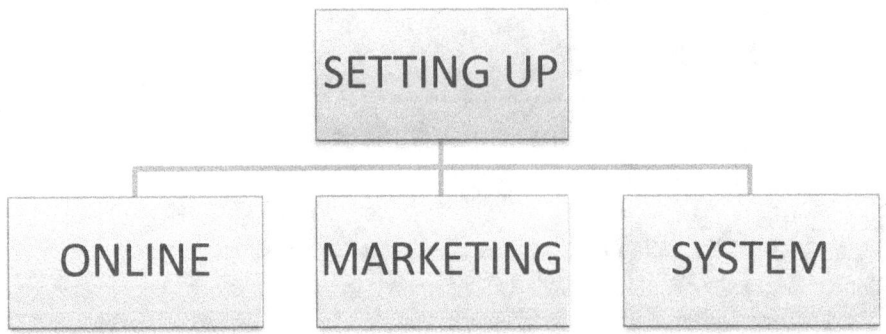

SETTING UP

ONLINE | MARKETING | SYSTEM

The past should not hold back YOUR progress in the present and the FUTURE.

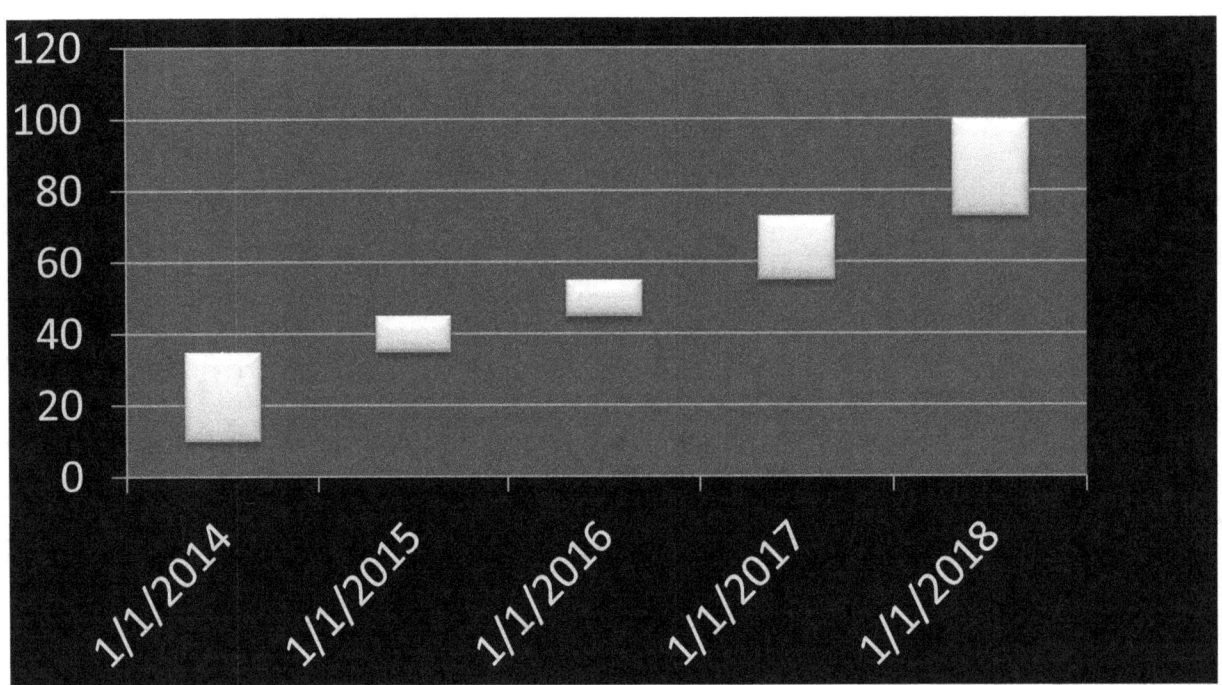

Time Does What Your Effort Can't DO

- When you understand what Affiliate Marketing requires. Then Time does the rest.

- Online marketing is a clear written success in the minds of those that follow Time, work with Time, save Time and allow Time to act.

- You've read through this Article and have acquired the knowledge of Headline writing and Ads

- Generating Traffic is based on your online system and the conversion into success by Time

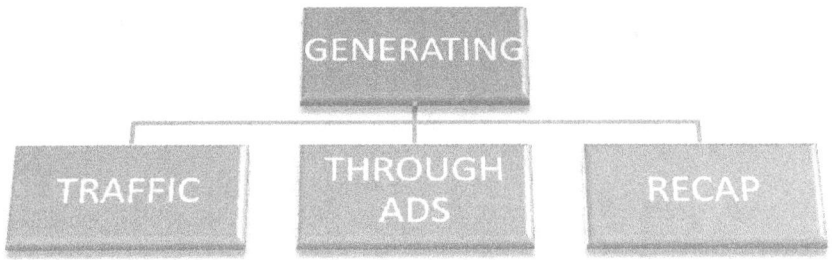

- All the above listed Methods of Generating Paid or Free Traffic or creating the awareness/selling of your products/services boil down to the following:
- Social Networking :– [FaceBook, Twitter, LinkedIn, MoboFree, Etc]
- Personal Networking :-[to exchange information, ideas, advice, contacts, and support]
- Creating a Website that is Functional, Easy to NAVIGATE and ACTIVE
- Primary Publicity :– [Lectures on your product or services, granting interviews, billboard posts, etc. relating to Advance Media Relations]
- Advanced Media Relations: – [creating the awareness of your product or services publicly, using images, newspapers, TV, etc.]
- Direct Marketing: – [selling or advertising direct to the end customers – use of catalogue, email, telephone, etc.]
- Personal Marketing :– [advertising/selling or creating the awareness personally :– one on one basis]
- Awards: – [This is like Viral Marketing – give out your products/services Free to group of people and so on. Offer Discounts, recognizing your regular customers]
- Trade Shows/Fair/Events :– [This explains itself; making your products available for Trade Shows, Trade Fair or Events]
- **Read more related** <u>Articles Here!</u>

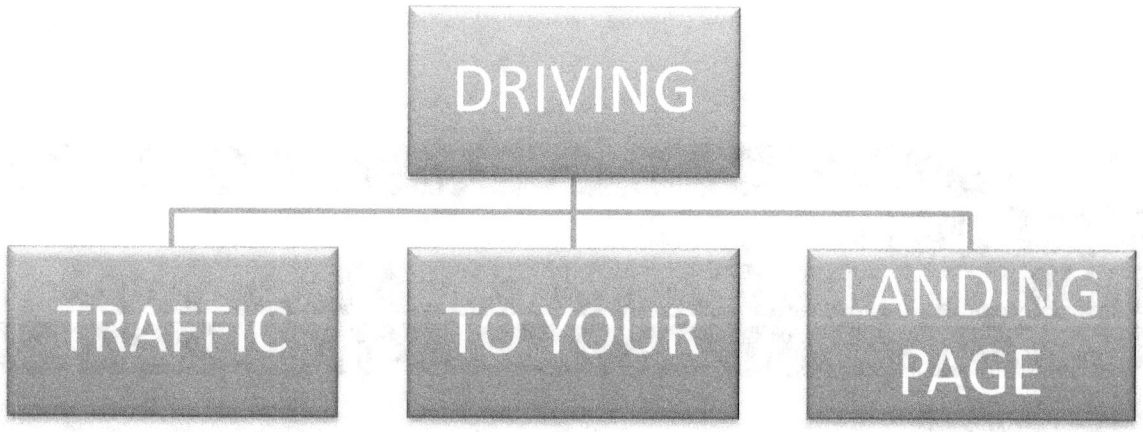

- **Driving Traffic To Your Landing Page, Does It Really Matter?**

- **Direct Linking and Landing Page – Who Benefits More?**

- There are many things that produce success online, if done in the rightful way.

- You must have heard that **TRAFFIC** is the soul of Online business right! Yes.. We discussed it previously

- And you must have also heard that without **TRAFFIC**, your website is **WEAK and DEAD**. Certain!

- All of these are facts that everyone in this industry has to consider when planning his or her Campaign.

When starting Online Marketing Business, Driving Traffic is often the major problem.

Having a website or products or services might not be difficult.

But bringing in the real Traffic your website or product needs is often cumbersome.

As an Affiliate, how do you Drive or Generate TRAFFIC?

Do you use the Direct Method/Linking – sending traffic direct to the Merchant's Web Page? Or

Landing Page – sending traffic to your campaign [Your Website] before directing it to the Merchant's Web Page?

Which one pays handsomely?

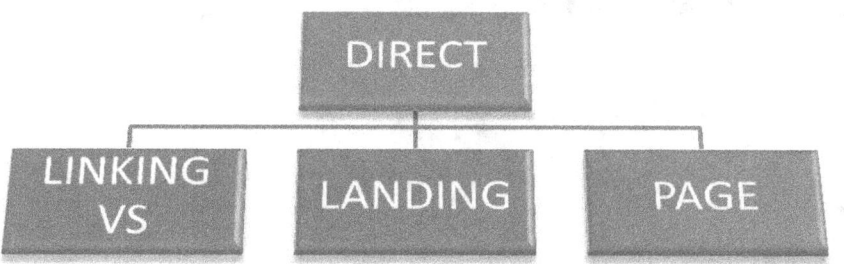

Simple format on direct linking

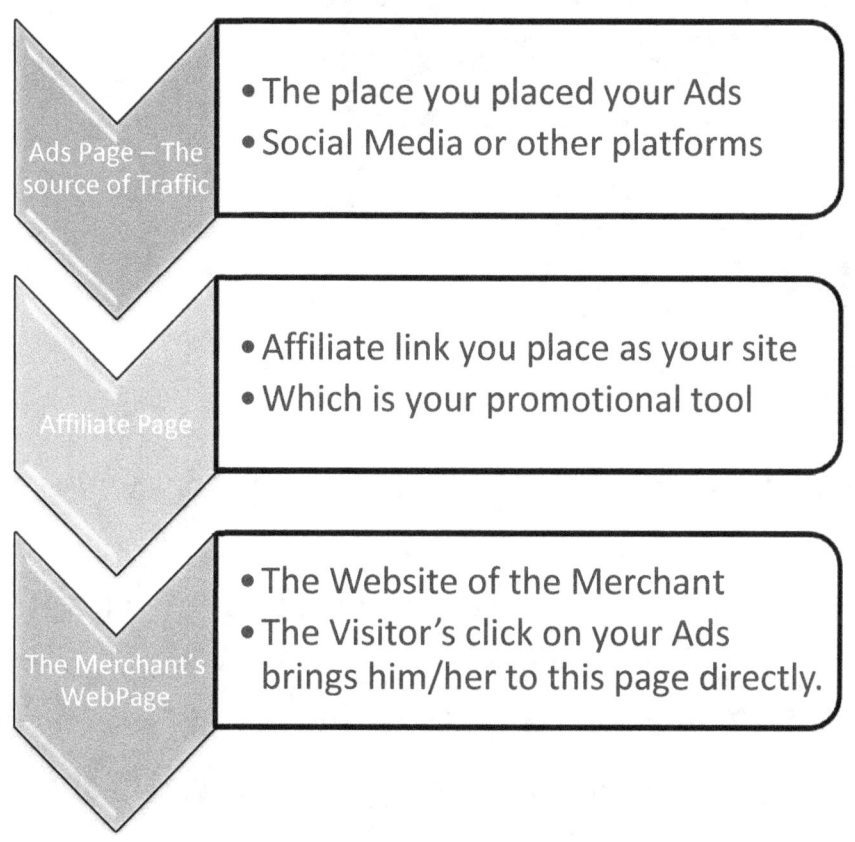

Ads Page – The source of Traffic
- The place you placed your Ads
- Social Media or other platforms

Affiliate Page
- Affiliate link you place as your site
- Which is your promotional tool

The Merchant's WebPage
- The Website of the Merchant
- The Visitor's click on your Ads brings him/her to this page directly.

Then, the merchant makes the sells and also gets the customer's details – the name and email and phone number where possible.

Simple format on Landing page

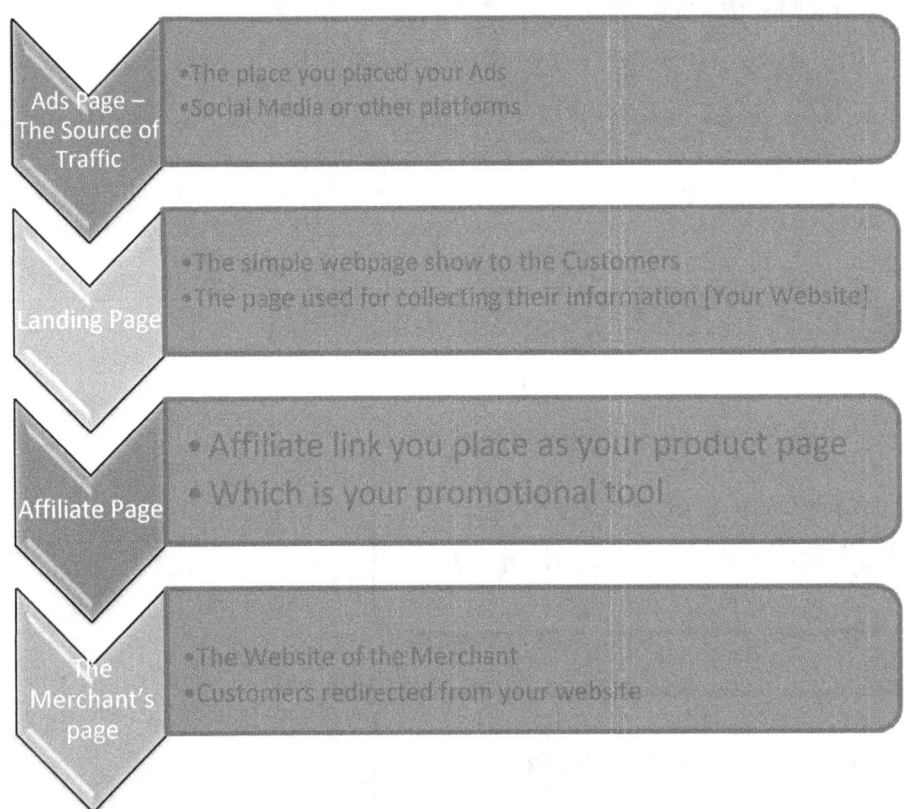

Ads Page – The Source of Traffic
- The place you placed your Ads
- Social Media or other platforms

Landing Page
- The simple webpage show to the Customers
- The page used for collecting their information [Your Website]

Affiliate Page
- Affiliate link you place as your product page
- Which is your promotional tool

The Merchant's page
- The Website of the Merchant
- Customers redirected from your website

As an Affiliate, having a list of your own is the best thing that will happen to you in this industry. Though you will see thousands of people that will tell you, it does not matter. Without your own list it will always be difficult for you to have power over your product or services. You might toil for years, placing Ads everywhere but the returns will be lower than your expenses. So Driving Traffic to Your Landing Page is the best way to build your list.

How Do You Drive Traffic To Your Landing Page? - In this case, you will be directing traffic from any Ads network to your webpage first, usually collecting their name and email and phone numbers wher necessary, and then directing the visitor to the merchant's webpage.

Importance Of Driving Traffic To Your Landing Page

- This is VERY lucrative...and is EXTREMEMLY valuable in creating a LONG TERM business. Because once you have an email list...you can continue to market products and services to those people well into the future.

- Creating a list is one of the facts that make Affiliate Marketing Interesting. It's HUGELY important...in a lot of cases, campaigns that you aren't able to make profitable with Direct Linking...you can be more profitable by first **Driving Traffic to your Landing Page**, building a list, and then directing that traffic to the affiliate offer you're promoting. The customer/visitor long term value is just so much higher when they are a part of your newsletter.

- Sending email any time to your LIST on a new product or service patterning your Niche will be so easy. And others can leverage your LIST either through Solo Ads or Email Swaps, all are profits, profits and Profits.

How To Spot A Good Landing Page

- Basically, our Landing Page is met accidentally by the customers or visitors while surfing the NET.

- It is Most Important that our LANDING PAGE should be short, captivating, and to the point.

- It has to explain briefly what your product or service has to offer to the visitor or customer.

- So usually, what works very well is REVIEWING the **Landing Pages** of the top products within our niche, seeing what type of copy they use, words on the page, and then making our own landing page based on that.

HOW TO DEVELOP A LANDING PAGE

- Let's see how it works best using the exact words from the webpage/product you're advertising.

- I personally like Health & Fitness Programs so I have to build a **Landing Page** base on the Merchant's Product.

- Through Clickbank, it is easy to promote products. Once you sign up to clickbank, you have thousand and one products you can promote base on your niche.

- Let's go to the ClickBank's MarketPlace for the Product.

- If you have not Signed Up yet, click Here www.clickbank.com

- You will be taken to Clickbank Home Page, Click on Sign Up then this Form below will appear:-

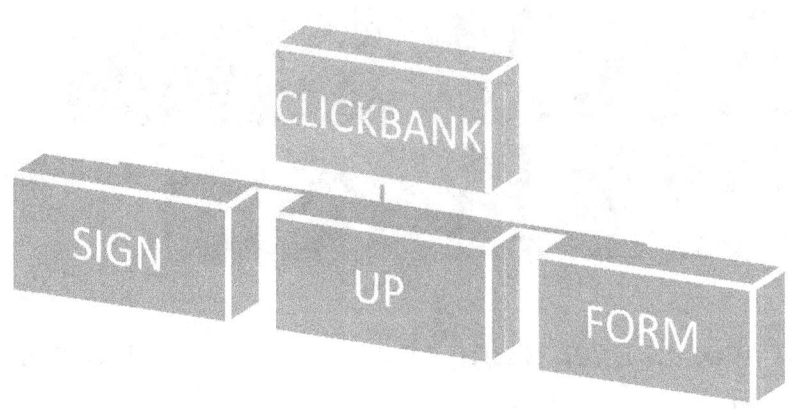

Home | Sign Up | Marketplace | Order Help | Blog | Log in   search

CLICKBANK

Sell Products   **Promote Products**   Buy Products   About Us   Help Center

Aide / Hilfe / Ayuda

ClickBank Signup Form

Use your mouse, or *tab* and *shift* tab to move from blank to blank.

                                                              * Required

Where shall we send your checks?

Country:*   UNITED STATES

Payee Name:*

Street / PO Box:*

Suite or Apt #:

City:*

State / Province: ALABAMA

Zip / Post Code:*

How can we contact you?

Your first name:*

Your last name:*

Your email address (example: joe@aol.com):*

Email address confirmation:*

Your phone number (required!):*   ext:

Address of your Web site (if any):

Select an account nickname for your new account

Account Nickname # (5-10 letters & digits):*

Check here to receive targeted, account specific
promotions from ClickBank via email

After filling the Form as you desired it to be, then you have to submit it.
Click on Submit to complete your Sign Up.
Another Page will appear for the confirmation of your Email Address.
The next page will look like this below.

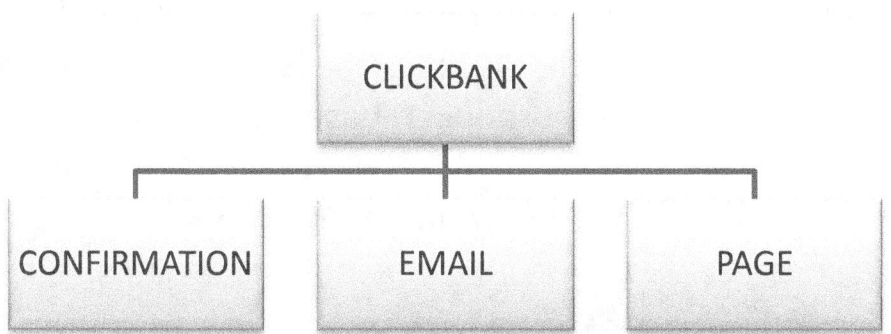

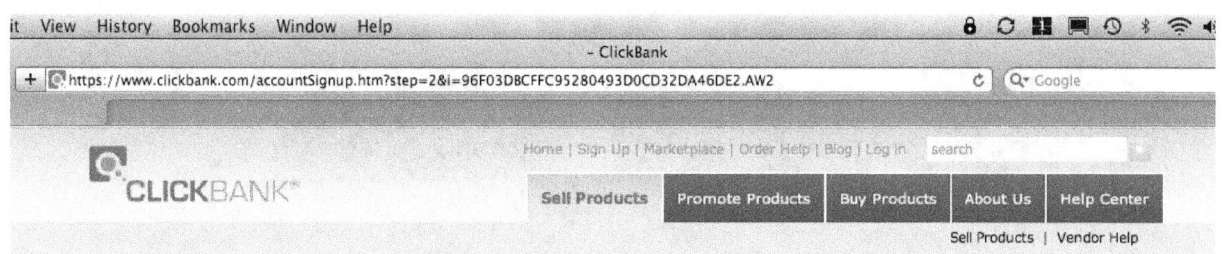

Signup Not Yet Complete

A signup completion link and 8 digit "confirmation code" have been emailed to you.

Please check your email and **click the link** to complete the process.

NOTE: If you do not receive our email within five minutes, it is because either your email program or your email provider has filtered it out as possible spam. You should take steps now to correct that problem.

© 2010 ClickBank :: Contact Us :: Legal & Policies :: Press :: Referral Program :: Sitemap

Now go to your email that you used in ClickBank Form to check the mail sent to your box. Get the Confirmation Code and then click on the Confirmation Link on that mail. Then a 'Thank You' Page will be the next thing you will see. It is time to start your Promotion. The Marketplace is the next thing you have to click to promote a product base on Your Niche. Like I said earlier, I love Health & Fitness. So base on that Category I will find the product to promote.

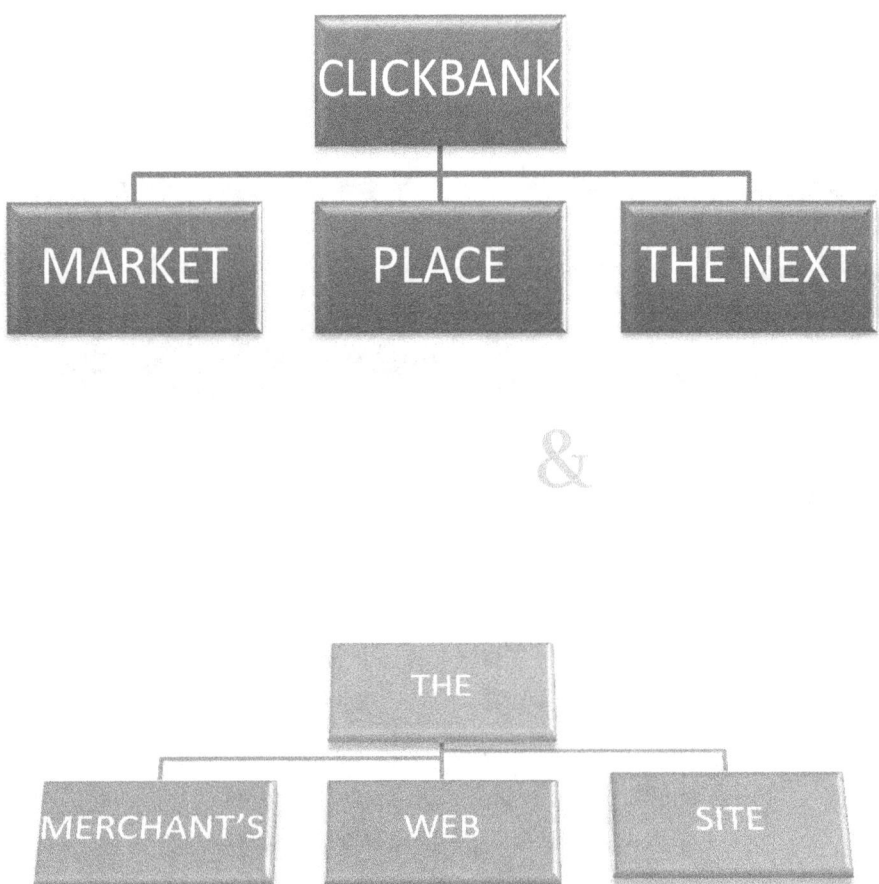

ClickBank Market Place

The Merchant's Site

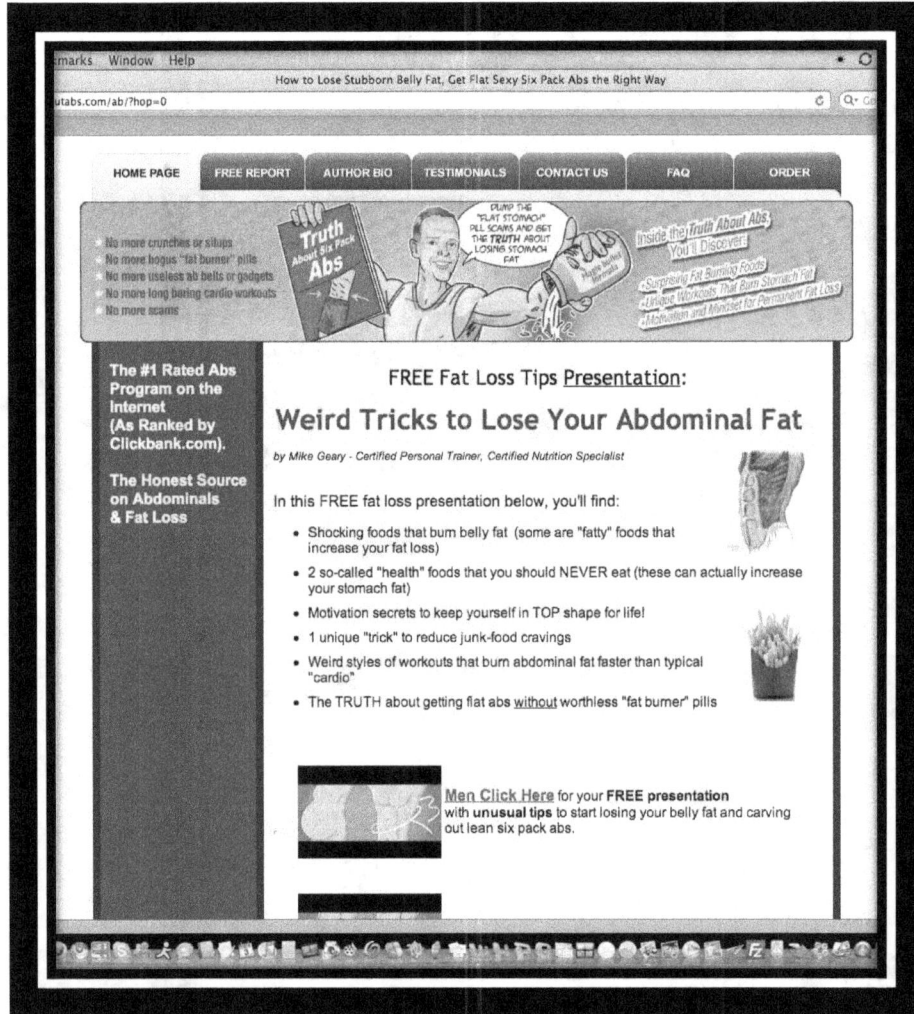

This Merchant's Webpage has all I need to create a beautiful Landing Page.

It has in detail the information any one searching for <u>Fat Burn or Weight loss</u> will like to hear. And also it has the bullet points which makes it more easier for me to create my landing page.
So My Landing Page Will Be Like This Blow:-

• "Weird TRICKS to Lose Your Abdominal Fat"

- In this You'll Learn:

- Taking the confusion out of healthy eating

- Unconventional workout ideas

- Nutrition tips for muscle building and fat loss

- Fitness motivation and a success mindset

- Healthy meals and recipes for a lean body

- Shocking foods that burn belly fat (some are "Fatty" foods that increase your fat loss)

- 2 so - called "Health" foods that you should NEVER eat (they can actually increase your stomach fat)

- 1 Unique "TRICK" to reduce junk-food cravings

- Weird styles of workouts that burn abdominal fat faster than typical "Cardio"

- The TRUTH about getting flat abs WITHOUT worthless <u>"Fat Burner"</u> pills

- And Many More!

- You'll also get the secrets of the following:

- [Healing Your Joints, Supercharging Your Energy][Naturally Fight the Aging Process] [Boost Your Metabolism, Fix Your Digestion][Protect Your Brain Health, Kill Blood Pressure]

- Just Enter your name and email. Your information is completely secured.
- First Name: [   ]   Email: [   ]
- Click [Instant Access] to Get Your Abdominal Fat Burn, Nutrition & Workout Programs. Allow the next page a few seconds to load.
- Be Strong, Be Active, Be Fit

This Landing Page has a captivating Headline, Body/Content and Call To Action [CTA]. Easily; those visitors in need of what I am offering will give their names and email addresses, then I would direct then to the Merchant's website. It's a perfect set up for the visitor and me, because everything that they just saw on the Landing Page before entering their names and emails in order to receive – they will get on the next page [which is the Merchant's Webpage]. That also makes me on the safer side, because it will lead to Trust. And I will build my Email list through this means. So with this, driving traffic to your landing page is often the best because you'll have a LIST to fall on all the time.

Get Your eBook Here!
Subscribe To Clickbank University and Build your Success Online. You Need Time To Work.

Time! Time!! TIME!!!

- What is the Meaning of Time to You? Maybe it is:

- **System for distinguishing events – which you use to measuring the occurrence of two events in interval at the same space of time**

- **Period with Limits – which all your efforts come to end with specific results. Or**

- **Period with No Limit – which brings all your efforts, decision, action and passion to a running over Success with no end.**

Every effort we give in a job or work has its own rightful time. Time constructs the space that success fills. But when we fail to understand the sentences of time, things become impossible to us. The mountain seems not climbable, the river swells higher than the ocean, the hill cripples the strength of the walking feet and the valley turns to the deepest pit. There is nothing like failure to one who takes Time to work. Such is always ahead of others because he or she puts and uses Time in different methods or ways to achieve his or her dreams.

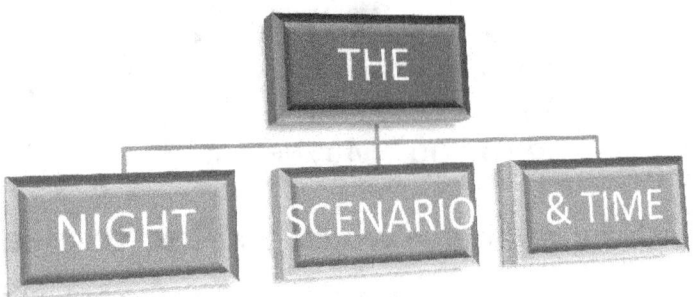

- I needed water to prepare my dish for the next morning, the tap runs a drop at a time 'tom, tom, tom'.

- I became confused and impatient about the situation then a thought came in.

- 'Why don't you put the bucket under the tap before morning, you will certainly have water you need.' I said, 'Oh that's a very long time to wait.'

- 'Give it a try and go to bed before morning you will be surprised.' My Inner man reprimanded.

- Quickly I put it under the tap, the first drop 'tom', followed the second 'tom'. I went out to do other things.

- Could you believe before morning I had bucket filled with water? I had much water than I wanted, which my effort couldn't do.

- How happy I was seeing that time has turned the drop of waters into a bucket of water.

- Time is the key success online marketing business. When you set your time well, the system or the program you're running will turn that time to success.

- Time is very important if you must succeed in your endeavors.

All you have to do is to set that you're doing right; give Time a chance to do the work for you and the success results would surely follow.

Allowing time act gives the work positive returns. We often destroy things that could yearn much in future because we refuse to allow patience and time to act in the place where our efforts are weak.

Online Marketing game has been the modernized business made easy for everyone. No language barrier, education, social status or what have you required but TIME covers all. Also; the knowledge of using the internet plays key roll. And lastly; the ability to neutralize information; works with TIME.

Knowledge is meaning less when people cannot make use of it. Time for change in your online business has come.

After all effort fixed; a system set up well, and then Time does the work for you. Be sure you have the right System set up and watch Time do the magic for you. Ebook Here!

Clickbank System Setup

Now Take All You Have Learnt So Far and Put Them In Practice.

Be Cautious To Follow The Right Path.

'Hard I Know' Is Often The Cry Of One That Despises Good Advise.

Save YourSelf From Failure Today!!

ONLINE MARKETING CURATOR – **THE TRAFFIC SOURCE:** IS FOR YOUR ONLINE SUCCES. **TAKE IT.** READ IT. MAKE USE OF IT. AND BUILD YOUR SUCCESS THROUGH IT. *The past year might not be as you expected, but look into the future with this GRAPH and achieve your dreams.*

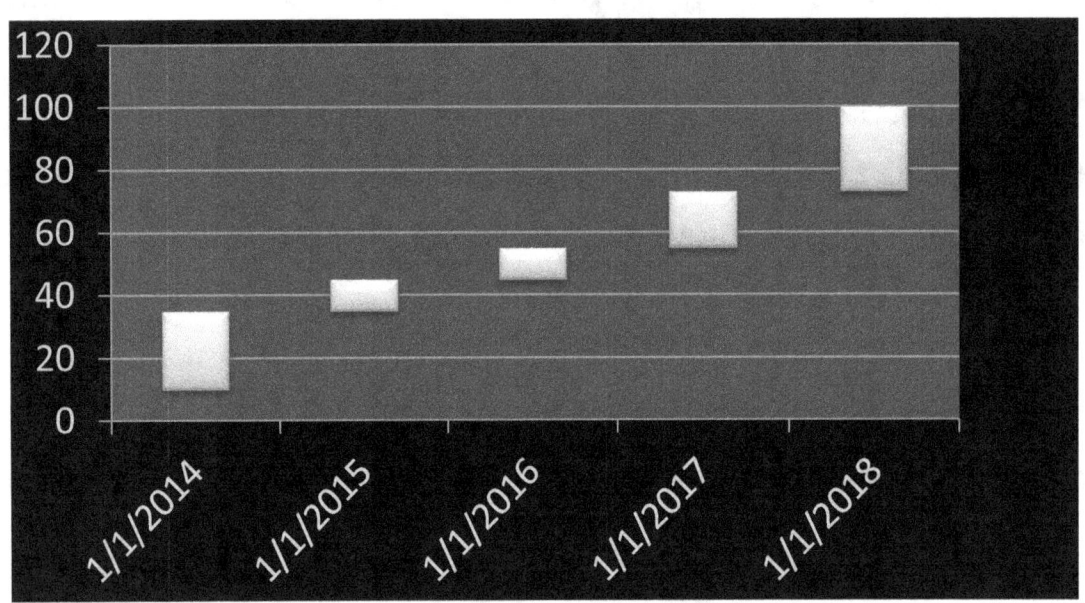

www.ingramcontent.com/pod-product-compliance
Lightning Source LLC
Chambersburg PA
CBHW080836180526
45168CB00006B/2710